THE PRESIDENTIAL SEAL

OFFICIAL SYMBOL OF THE PRESIDENT

JINNOW KHALID

PowerKiDS press
New York

Published in 2021 by The Rosen Publishing Group, Inc.
29 East 21st Street, New York, NY 10010

Portions of this work were originally authored by Walter LaPlante and published as *The Presidential Seal*. All new material in this edition authored by Jinnow Khalid.

Editor: Elizabeth Krajnik
Book design: Reann Nye

Photo Credits: Cover, p.1 SAUL LOEB/AFP/Getty Images; Series Art sunwart/Shutterstock.com; p. 5 Drew Angerer/Getty Images News/Getty Images; p. 7 https://commons.wikimedia.org/wiki/File:Declaration_of_Independence_(1819),_by_John_Trumbull.jpg; p. 9 Bloomberg/Getty Images; p. 11 https://commons.wikimedia.org/wiki/File:US_presidential_seal_1850.png; pp. 13–19 https://commons.wikimedia.org/wiki/File:Seal_of_the_President_of_the_United_States.svg; p. 21 Max Mumby/Indigo/Getty Images News/Getty Images.

Cataloging-in-Publication Data

Names: Khalid, Jinnow.
Title: The presidential seal: official symbol of the president / Jinnow Khalid.
Description: New York : PowerKids Press, 2021. | Series: America's favorite symbols | Includes glossary and index.
Identifiers: ISBN 9781725317260 (pbk.) | ISBN 9781725317284 (library bound) | ISBN 9781725317277 (6 pack)
Subjects: LCSH: Emblems, National–United States–Juvenile literature. | Seals (Numismatics)–United States–Juvenile literature. | Presidents–United States–Juvenile literature. | United States–Seal–Juvenile literature.
Classification: LCC CD5610.K475 2021 | DDC 929.9–dc23

Manufactured in the United States of America

CPSIA Compliance Information: Batch #CSPK20 For Further Information contact Rosen Publishing, New York, New York at 1-800-237-9932

CONTENTS

Symbol of the Presidency

The presidential **seal** is a **symbol** of the presidency. It's used on letters from the president to Congress and on other papers he or she signs **representing** the United States. You can see the presidential seal in many places—even on the carpet in the White House!

SEAL OF THE PRESIDENT OF THE UNITED STATES
E PLURIBUS UNUM

A New Nation

On July 4, 1776, the 13 colonies **declared** their **independence** from Great Britain and created a new nation—the United States of America. That evening, Congress said a seal for the new nation was needed. A seal is a symbol of the power of the government.

The Coat of Arms

The obverse, or front side, of the U.S. Great Seal is the **coat of arms** of the United States. The coat of arms is used on many important papers from the U.S. government, on U.S. money, and on government buildings throughout the United States.

Presidential Seal

The presidential seal is based on the coat of arms on the obverse of the Great Seal. In 1850, President Millard Fillmore drew the first **documented** presidential seal. Over the years, people made many changes to the presidential seal.

THE SEAL OF THE PRESIDENT OF THE UNITED STATES

Important Changes

In 1945, President Harry Truman made important changes to the seal. The eagle was changed to always face the olive branch and a circle of 48 stars was added. In 1959 and again in 1960, a star was added to the circle when Alaska and Hawaii became states.

SEAL OF THE PRESIDENT OF THE UNITED STATES
E PLURIBUS UNUM

The Eagle

The presidential seal has a bald eagle, the national bird of the United States, with wings outstretched. It's facing its right wing. The eagle holds a white scroll that reads "E pluribus unum," which means "out of many, one" in Latin.

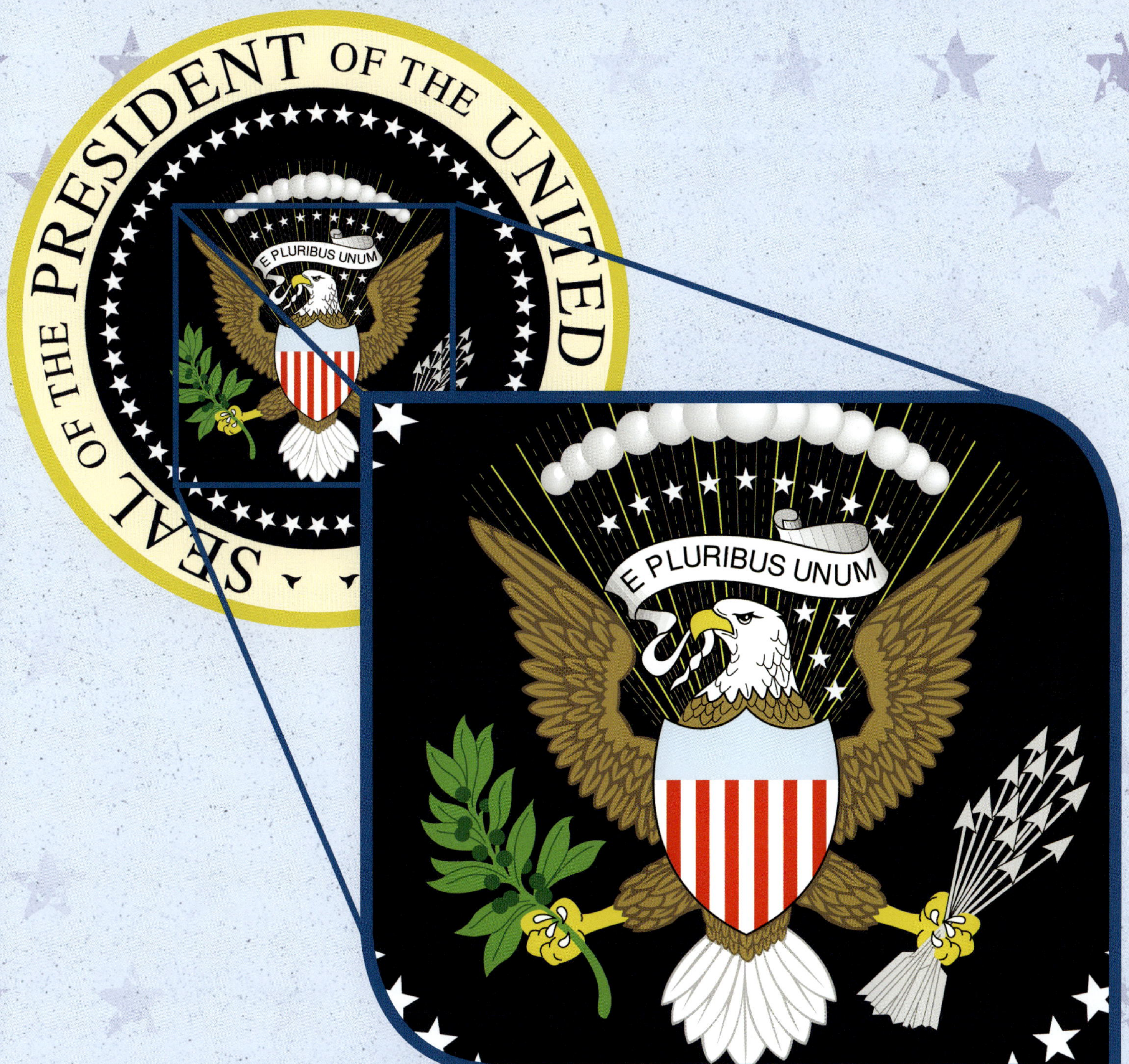
SEAL OF THE PRESIDENT OF THE UNITED
E PLURIBUS UNUM
E PLURIBUS UNUM

In the eagle's dexter (right) talons, or claws, it holds an olive branch with 13 leaves and 13 olives. This represents peace. In its sinister (left) talons, the eagle holds 13 arrows. This represents the need to sometimes go to war.

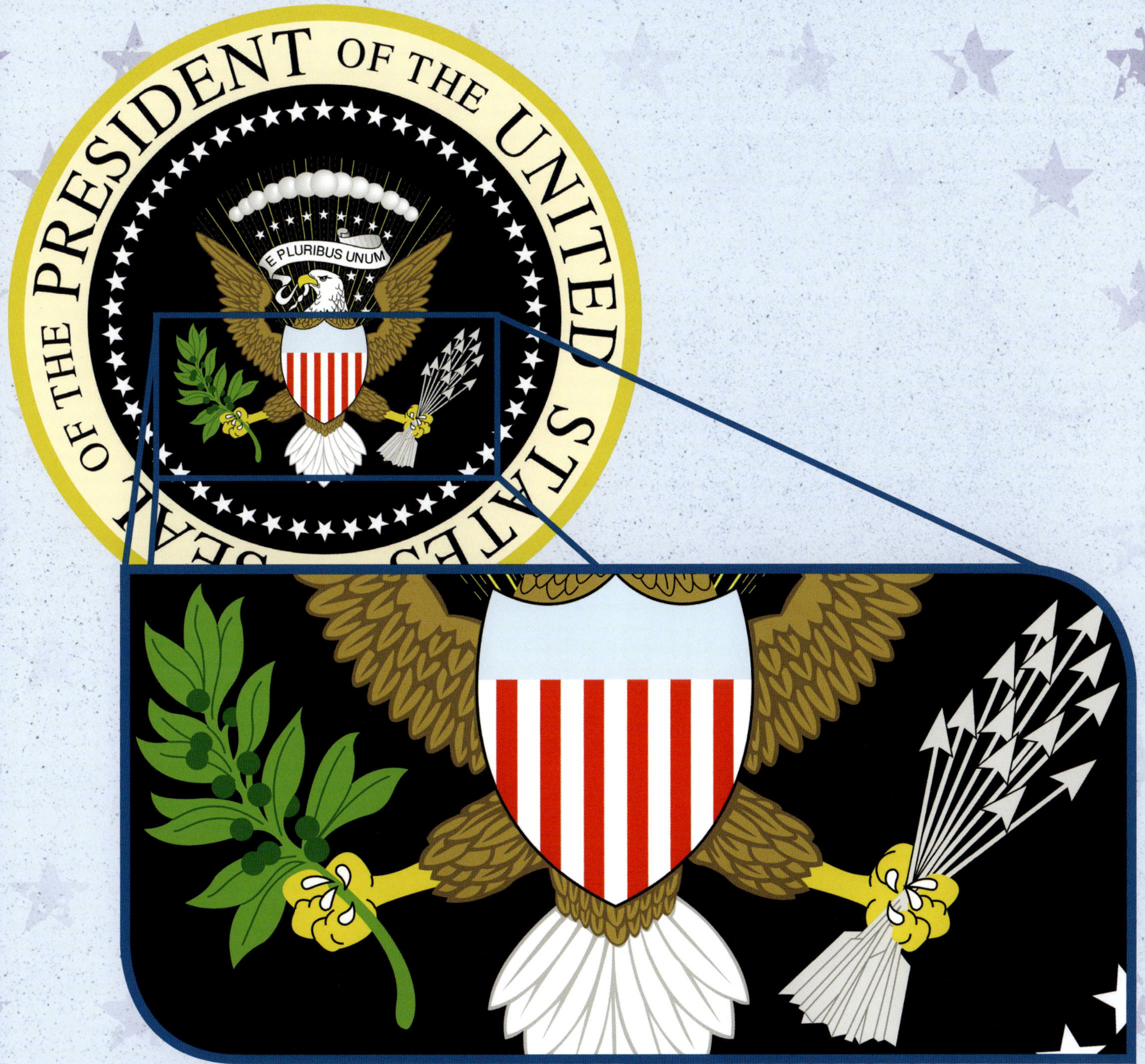
SEAL OF THE PRESIDENT OF THE UNITED STATES
E PLURIBUS UNUM

The Shield

The shield covering the eagle's body has 13 gules (red) and argent (silver) pales (up-and-down stripes). These represent the 13 original colonies. They sit under an azure (blue) chief (side-to-side stripe). This represents the unity of the colonies into one nation and Congress, which makes the nation's laws.

SEAL OF THE PRESIDENT OF THE UNITED
E PLURIBUS UNUM

Stars and States

The presidential seal's eagle is on a blue background ringed by 50 stars, which represent the 50 states. The stars are surrounded by the words "Seal of the President of the United States." Above the eagle are 13 clouds and 13 stars.

SEAL OF THE PRESIDENT OF THE UNITED STATES
E PLURIBUS UNUM

Timeline

July 4, 1776
Congress declares the United States an independent nation and calls for a national seal to be made.

September 15, 1789
Congress adopts the Great Seal. The presidential seal is based on the obverse of the Great Seal.

1850
President Millard Fillmore draws the first documented presidential seal.

1945
President Harry Truman changes the eagle to always face toward the olive branch and adds the outer ring of 48 stars.

1959
A 49th star is added to the seal to represent Alaska.

1960
A 50th star is added to the seal to represent Hawaii.

GLOSSARY

coat of arms: A special group of pictures or symbols belonging to a person, family, or group and shown on a shield.

declare: To say or state something in an official or public way.

document: To record (as on paper) the details about something.

independence: Freedom from outside control or support.

represent: To be a sign or symbol of something.

seal: An official mark stamped or pressed on something.

symbol: Something that stands for something else.

INDEX

WEBSITES

Due to the changing nature of Internet links, PowerKids Press has developed an online list of websites related to the subject of this book. This site is updated regularly. Please use this link to access the list: www.powerkidslinks.com/afs/presseal